En esta foto que tomé en 1960
presentí en su mirada la
frase de su carta de despedida a Fidel
..."hasta la victoria siempre".

Korda.

Ernestito

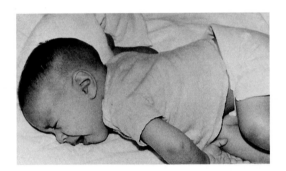

On June 14, 1928, Ernesto Guevara Lynch and Celia de la Serna y Llosa proudly announce the birth of their first child. In true Argentinean fashion, they name him after his father. Born one month before term at Rosario de la Fe, the newborn is also given two nicknames: "Ernestito" and "Tete."

An explosive mixture of Irish, Spanish, and Basque blood runs in Ernestito's veins. His mother, Celia, is the heiress of a family of landowners related to Spanish and New World nobility. As a pretty, rebellious young woman, she embraces feminism as early as the end of the first World War.

In Buenos Aires, Latin America's most European capital, she is one of the first women to create a public scandal by cutting her hair short. She drives her own car, signs her own checks, and "crosses her legs in public," reveals one of her female cousins.

Celia sets her heart on a young man from her social circle. Ernesto Guevara Lynch seems to her the least arrogant and narrow-minded of all her suitors. Handsome and kind, he has inherited his love of traveling from a grandfather who, when forced into exile, took it as an opportunity to join the California gold rush. Ernesto Guevara Lynch can't stand working behind a desk. Giving up his studies in architecture, he takes his wife and baby to the northeast where he exploits the plantations of mate, an herb used in making the most popular drink in Argentina and Paraguay.

Ernestito spends his years in an immense garden.

Then a considerable influence

4

first two

n 1930, an event occurs which will have on his future character.

On May 2, the little boy catches cold while bathing in the icy waters of a swimming pool. His first asthma attack signals the beginning of a curse that is to help forge his iron will. One of the first words Ernestito learns to say is "injection." Under doctor's orders, the Guevaras leave the northeast in search of a healthier climate. They move to Alta Gracia, a city nestled in the mountains of the province of Cordoba, in northwest Argentina.

Alta grasia 12-16
querida Beatris resi-
bi tu carta y los cu:
atros libros yaora
no te por que lla di
aca ~~XXXXXXXX~~

resibe un abra
de
Ernestito

His mother teaches him to read at the age of four. Ernestito addresses his first letter to his aunt Beatriz, in 1933, at age five.

"The Guevaras left their house open to the public at all times," remembers a neighbor.

"Before they arrived, it was believed to be haunted. But with them, it became the house of the people. The neighborhood children were delighted. In fact, the parents encouraged Ernestito and his brothers and sisters, Celia, Roberto, Ana Maria and later Juan Martin, to invite all their friends to the house, regardless of whether they belonged to the same social class or sold newspapers."

Ernestito plays cowboys and indians like all children his age. But he also plays Francoists and republicans, a game of his times—it's 1936.

"*A real daredevil!,*" *his father later recalls. "At seven or eight, he was the ringleader of neighboring peons' children." But Ernestito also spends hours avidly reading all the books in the family library. "He would devour everything," continues Ernestito's "old man." "Of course, he began with Salgari. Then he moved on to Jules Verne, Cervantes, Stevenson. He was mad about adventure stories. The Three Musketeers . . ." His mother teaches him French, the traditional mark of Argentina's great families. At fourteen, he reads Baudelaire, Mallarmé, Pablo Neruda, Anatole France, and Jack London, as well as Freud, Jung, and an abridged version of* Das Capital.

Ernestito's 1945 class report card from the Dean Funes school in Cordoba: "A bright student . . . except in English!"

A passion for rugby springs from his encounter with the **Granado** brothers, especially Alberto, who later becomes his best friend.

Despite his asthma, which sometimes forces him to abandon the field, Ernesto earns the nickname "Fuser," an abbreviation of furibando ("furious") and Serna (his mother's maiden name). But his parents force him to quit the San Isidro de Buenos Aires rugby club. Obstinate as ever, he secretly joins another. With some friends, he creates the rugby magazine Tackle. Ernesto the reporter signs his first articles under still another of his nicknames: "Chancho" ("Pig") or "Chang-Cho."

A FALSE DILETTANTE

Affected by the suffering of his grandmother, who dies in 1947, Ernesto decides to study medicine at the University of Buenos Aires. Exempted from his national service because of asthma, the student plays tennis, golf and takes flying lessons with his uncle Jorge. But he also makes a point of earning a living.

He signs up as a nurse on a cargo ship, works in the municipal slaughterhouse, then in the university library. With a friend, he tries to produce an insecticide, Atila, which he hopes to manufacture commercially. The two young men only succeed in filling Ernesto's home with a foul odor.

"I don't know how he was able to do so many things. I have often thought that, despite his apparent lack of order, he was meticulously organised in everything that had to do with how he structured his time."
Ernesto Guevara, Senior.

13

University disappoints him.
He searches for a vocation but is
instead presented with a career.
Ernesto thirsts to discover the world.

During a university holiday, he decides to join Alberto
Granado in the Sierra, north of Cordoba. Older than
Ernesto, "Mial" (short for "Mi Alberto") has already
graduated from medical school and works in a leper
hospital at San Francisco de Chanar. To overcome
the 850-kilometer distance that separates them,
Ernesto attaches a small motor to his bicycle. His luggage
consists of a spare tire slung around his shoulders like a hunting horn, a few
clothes, and a book by Nehru.

El Grafico *magazine publishes a photo of Ernesto on May 5, 1950, as an*
advertisement for Cucciolo, the little motor's trademark.

"He went where people were the poorest and the neediest, as though he wished to absorb all the misery in his America in one blow."

Alfredo Reyes Trejo

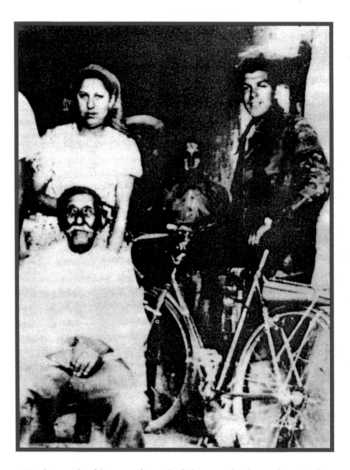

At the end of his working holiday at the leper hospital in San Francisco de Chanar, Ernesto returns to Buenos Aires, carefully avoiding the main roads. Along the way, he shares the life of the gauchos. Altogether, he covers 4,500 kilometers on the roads of Argentina.

Bolsa sud befe (Fuera)
1. Malla
2. Pullovers
2. Pantalons
1. Calzoncillo
     "
1. Camiseta
4. Comidas
2. para ...
2. por .
1. Cuchillo
1. Tenedor
1. Cuchara
1. fuente
1. Tapa aluminio
1. Cuchara
1. Bufanda
1. Necesser
1. Por montaña...
1. Par de zapatillas

1 Par de cuartos

Parilla
1. Parilla
1. Cárpa - 6 estivo
2. Catres
1. Bolsa
foco de cuero
Trafe azul
Trafe ...
Colchoa - 1 -
Calentador - 1
olla
Tongas 4 l.
Sufladors - 1
Mochan de ...
Saldados
... bosa

On the road...

At twenty-three, Ernesto has almost finished medical school. Possessed by an overwhelming desire for adventure, he decides to travel across Latin America by motorcycle with his friend, Alberto.

On December 29, 1951, the two friends climb onto an old Norton 500 cm3; they call it the Poderosa II *("powerful"). Behind them a barbecue grill sits atop sleeping bags, a tent, and some clothes. Their parents cannot hide their concern. Ernesto has to promise to always take his asthma medication and to return to finish his doctorate. Before their departure, his father slides a revolver into their belongings, just in case.*

Romantic interlude.

Their first stop is Miramar's elitist seaside resort, where Ernesto's girlfriend, Maria "Chichina" del Carmen, is staying. Chichina is the daughter of the baron Ferreira.

To the young scions of the Argentinean aristocracy Guevara seems about as sociable as a bear, and his comments fall on their ears like lead. To Chichina, however, his behavior is enchanting. "His disheveled appearance made us laugh but also rendered us a bit ashamed of our own submission to fashion. He bought his shoes at secondhand shops and chose them so to give the impression that his feet were two different sizes. He was completely oblivious to our snobbery."

"The voyage," writes Ernesto in his diary upon his departure, "is in the balance, in a cocoon, subordinate to the word which consents and ties."
As a farewell gift, Chichina presents him with a gold bracelet. He leaves her a little dog he has christened "Come Back."

expertos argentinos en leprol
corren Sudamérica en motoc

atán en Temuco y desean visitar Rapa-

Doctors of the world

On February 19, 1952, the local paper of Temuco, a small town in Chile, reports that, "two Argentinean leprosy experts are riding across South America by motorcycle."

Dr. Granado and his "associate," Guevara, cross the Andes cordillera, and reach Chile. Even at this early stage, the Norton is already suffering. They are forced to abandon it and hitchhike to Valparaiso where, as *polizones,* they illegally board a freighter bound for Bolivia. There, they visit the gigantic mines of Chuquicamata, exploited by North Americans. Injustice is revealed to them: "By a sleight of hand that went unnoticed by the Indians," Alberto recounted later, "their red earth transformed itself into green dollar bills."

The comrades continue toward Peru—Lake Titicaca, Cuzco, the Machu Picchu—then down the Amazon River to the leper colony of San Pablo. More than forty years later, the lepers still recall the two almost supernatural beings who shook their hands without gloves and played football with them. Silvio Lozano, who today owns a bar named "Che," confided in journalist Andy Dressler:

"In 1952, I was one of the many lepers condemned to die in a matter of months. I was nothing but a bag of bones. The disease was slowly eating away at me and the pain made me cry. Che sat on the floor beside me like a yogi. I was so weak, I couldn't even give him my hand. He took mine, inspected it thoroughly and then said: 'Your nerve is affected. We must operate!' Despite his cool hand on my burning forehead, I was struck by terror. 'You will die if we don't do anything,' he insisted. I screamed like a lunatic when I felt the needles prick my wounds. Then I sought his gaze and fainted. He saved my life. This marked the beginning of a new era for our community. The surgical instruments hadn't had time to rust."

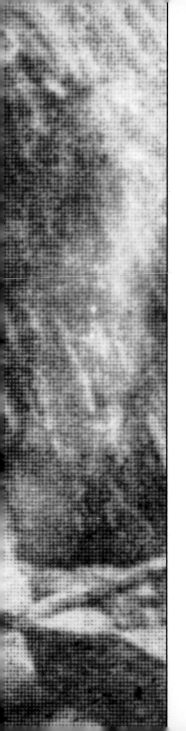

As a show of gratitude, the lepers build a raft with which Alberto and Ernesto continue their journey down the Amazon River. As the patients are Peruvian and the doctors Argentinean, the raft is christened *Mambo-Tango.*

"To say their good-byes, the patients formed a choir, illuminated by the flickering light of lanterns and torches. The accordion player had virtually no fingers on his right hand. In their place were bamboo sticks bound to his wrist. The singer was blind, and almost all of them were disfigured by the disease. The scene could have been part of a horror film but will remain one of my most beautiful memories."
While visiting the ruins at Machu Picchu, Ernesto ponders upon the misery of the Indians: "As a result of the conditions in which I travel, I have discovered that it is impossible to heal children who are ill due to poverty, malnutrition and constant repression."

SELF-PORTRAIT of Ernesto the photographer. His camera is on the left atop a pile of books.

At the end of July, 1952, after having traveled together for seven months, the two companions part ways in Caracas. Ernesto had a dollar left in his pocket and had promised his mother to return to finish medical school. The air freighter that takes him to Buenos Aires is forced to make a twenty-day stopover in Miami. He finds the United States in the throes of McCarthyism. Back in Argentina, he finishes his doctorate in record time, from September 1952 to March 1953. He is "Dr." Guevara before his twenty-fifth birthday, a title which he couldn't care less about. He longs to travel anew. The American continent merits a **"systematic political auscultation."**

He sets off for Peru again, staying a while in Bolivia, traveling through Ecuador and then Costa Rica, where he meets Cuban exiles who, on July 26, had just launched their first armed operation against the dictator Batista. The exiles speak of their leader, a certain Fidel Castro Ruz. He is in Guatemala when mercenaries backed by the CIA intervene to topple the progressive regime of President Arbenz. There he meets Hilda Gadea Acosta, a militant Peruvian exile.

She introduces him to the readings of Lenin, Trotski, and Mao. The lovers participate in the resistance, but have to flee to Mexico. With his new friend Julio Caceres, or "El Patojo," Ernesto survives by taking photographs of lovers or mothers taking their children for a walk in the park, **"struggling to convince them that the little boy really is adorable and worth the one peso for the memento."**

The press agency Latina employs him as their photographer for the Pan-American Games.

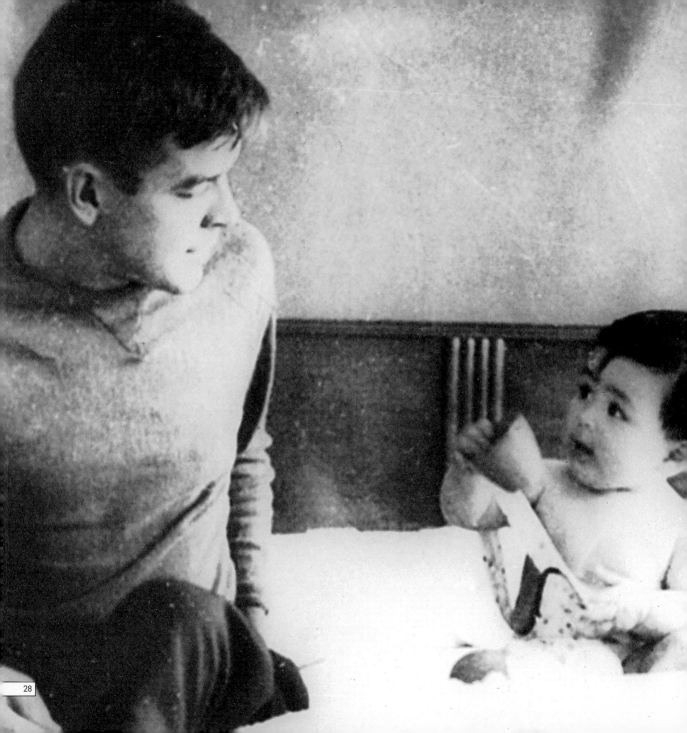

Ernesto's inspiration, Hilda Gadea, is pregnant. She finally accepts his marriage proposal in 1955, but their union quickly deteriorates. "I am expecting a little Vladimir Ernesto," Guevara writes to his aunt Beatriz a few months later. Instead, Hilda Beatriz is born. No matter. "My communist heart is bursting at the seams," writes Ernesto, this time to his mother. "She is the spitting image of Mao Zedong. She eats just the way Grandmother used to say I did, in other words, she sucks at her mother's breast until the milk spurts out of her nostrils." The young father calls his firstborn "El petalo mas profondo del amor."

However, the year 1955 is marked by an encounter which will have more influence on his destiny than his paternity. In Mexico, Ernesto Guevara meets the Cuban exiles' chief, Fidel Castro. He writes to his father, "A young Cuban leader has invited me to join his country's armed liberation movement, and I, of course, have accepted. My future is therefore tied to the Cuban revolution. . . . I have gone through life seeking my truth in fits and starts and now that I'm on my way and have a daughter who will live after me, I have closed the cycle. **From now on, do not consider my death as a frustration for, like Hikmet, I will only take to the grave the regret of an unfinished song. . . ."**

Castro is in search of a doctor for the group of revolutionaries he plans to send to Cuba to overthrow the dictator Batista.

Guevara doesn't hesitate one second. His Cuban friends nickname him, "Che," the Argentineans' favorite interjection which distinguishes them from other Latin Americans.

Under the orders of Colonel Bayo, a former officer of the Spanish Republican Army, "Che" Guevara trains at marksmanship with the Cubans in a secret camp about 40 kilometers from Mexico.

Fidel Castro, Ernesto Gueva*r*

and the group of Cuba

in Mexico's Miguel Schu

They are later rele
of the former Presi

ORDENAN

que salgan de México
cubanos libertados;
Castro sigue preso

MEXICO, julio 11. (UP). —El
Ministerio del Interior anunció
que sólo quedan detenidas tres
personas por la acusación de
conspirar contra el gobierno del
presidente Batista, de Cuba. Los
detenidos son el doctor Castro
Ruz (Fidel), el médico argenti-
no Guevara Serna y el cubano
García Martínez.

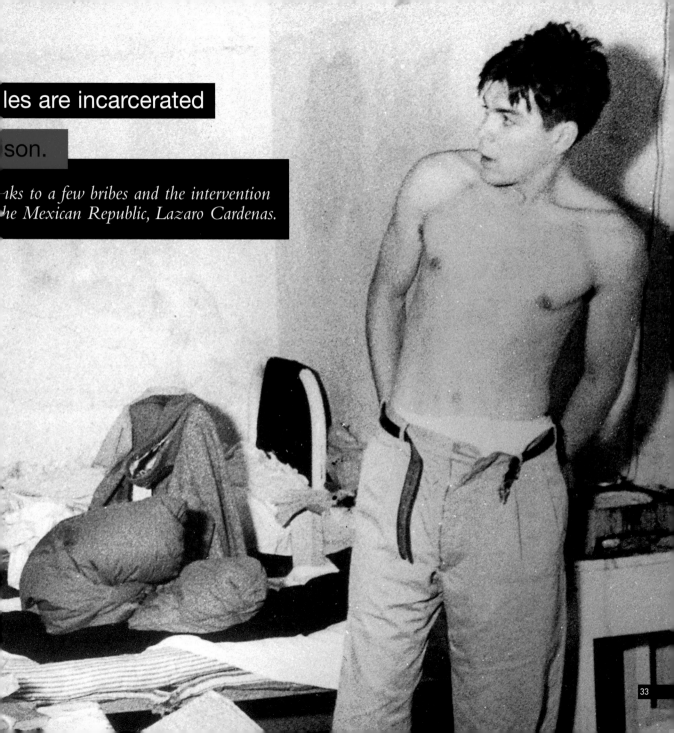

les are incarcerated

son.

...nks to a few bribes and the intervention ...he Mexican Republic, Lazaro Cardenas.

Before confronti

"Che" strive

To his mother: *"I am neither a Christ nor a philanthropist. I am everything contrary to a Christ, and philanthropy seems worthless in comparison to what I believe in. I will fight with all the weapons within my reach rather than let myself be nailed to a cross or whatever."*

...he primitive life of a guerrilla,

...o turn his body into a fighting machine.

His life no longer belongs to him. He has pledged it to the Revolution. With his Cuban comrades, he does wrestling and karate for hand-to-hand combat, basketball and football for agility, and rowing for endurance. He spends his weekends climbing Mount Popocatepetl or Mount Iztaccihuatl, which top out at more than 5,000 meters. Fidel travels to the United States in order to collect funds from the exiles there.

On November 25, 1956, they and eighty Cubans board the *Granma*, a yacht built to transport only twenty-five passengers. Guevara is fully aware that his departure will separate him, perhaps permanently, from his nine-month-old daughter.

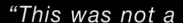

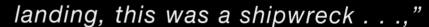

"This was not a landing, this was a shipwreck . . .,"

Che will say later on.

The eighty-two men landing on the Cuban coast on December 2, 1956, are decimated during their first confrontations with the regular army. The dozen survivors hide in the Sierra Maestra, an eighty miles long by thirty-one miles wide massif overlooked by the Turquino Mountain's peak lost in the clouds. Facing a modern army of a thousand men, the *Barbudos,* or Bearded men, learn their job. Slovenly-looking and armed to kill, they befriend local peasants, the Campesinos, who progressively come and swell their ranks.

Che trades his

38

In the midst of gunfire, "I had a knapsack filled with medicine and a case full of bullets in front of me. They were too heavy for me to carry them both. I picked up the case of bullets, leaving the knapsack behind . . ."

"This is a guerilla artist," said Fidel Castro, "a chief just as demanding with himself as he is with others. He practices an egalitarian doctrine which brings meaning to fighting against a dictatorship of corrupt individuals."

"This doctor is *Cojonudo* ("bloody brilliant"), a true warrior" says Fidel Castro.

Of an impulsive nature, he (Che) learns how to gain control over himself

in order to lead his troops

and to become a real *comandante* (commander).

In between being ambushed, he cares for the sick and the wounded. He tutors the illiterates and teaches French to Raul, the brother of Fidel Castro.

The Barbudos consume cigars in large quantities. They smoke a portion of the cigar, and as Ernesto taught them, let the rest soak in water. Once applied onto the skin, the yellowish liquid thus obtained is a powerful protection against mosquitoes.

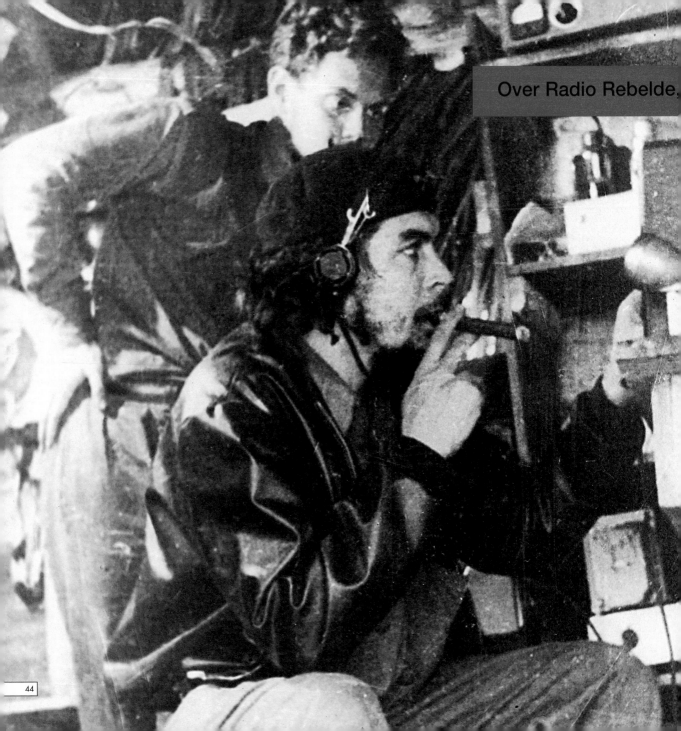

Guevara is named commander, the highest rank given by the guerilleros. Confined to his bed by an asthma attack, Che rereads Goethe in his fortified hideout at El Hombuto, which the army later reduces to ashes. He rebuilds a new permanent base in La Mesa. His men install a transmitter there and a printing press for their newspaper, El Cubano Libre. Over the airwaves and across the printed page, the message is simple: FREEDOM OR DEATH.

Commander Guevara creates a veritable weapons factory that specializes in the manufacture of bullets, grenades, and even a homemade weapon, the M26, also known as Sputnik, that is launched by a kind of catapult made from parts of a spear gun.

Within the "free zone" that they dominate and govern, the rebels pay for their purchases with coupons that Guevara already signs *Che*, as he will do when he becomes President of Cuba's National Bank, after the seizing of power.

On August 21, 1958, upon the order of Fidel Castro, the invasion of the rest of the island begins.
Across mountains and swamps, braving not only air raids but also two cyclones, Che travels several hundred kilometers on foot at the head of the *ocho,* a company of 220 men.

October 5: "The troop can't take any more. They are morally destitute, half-starved, and their feet are so bloody and swollen that they don't fit into their tattered shoes. A tiny light still glimmers in the depths of their desolate eyes. Walking amongst them, I felt the fervent desire to open my veins so that I could offer them something warm, something that they haven't had for the last three days, spent without food or sleep."

The two most famous and most wanted *Comandantes*: Che Guevara and his friend Camilo Cienfuegos.

On the road to Havana,
Santa Clara is Batista's last stronghold.
Che can count on only 364 men.

The army packs several thousand soldiers in a bulletproof train which the dictator considers his secret weapon against the revolution. The Barbudos sabotage the tracks, derailing the train. Protected by armour plating, the military open fire with their automatic weapons. Machine guns spit death from the turrets, but suicide commandos shower the train with Molotov cocktails. Its heavy, steel walls rapidly turn into a giant oven, forcing the trapped soldiers to surrender.

"*The woman is of great importance to the revolutionary process. She is capable of realizing the most difficult tasks, of fighting alongside the men. . . . To the primitive life of battle, she brings qualities characteristic of her sex and works just as hard as a man . . . but with a tenderness superior to that of her brothers in arms. Tenderness, how important you are in moments of suffering!*"

One night, while making his way back to his barracks by walking on rooftops, Che slips and falls. A television antenna gashes his temple and he sprains a wrist. Afraid of an allergic reaction, he refuses the nurse's anesthesia. Arm in a sling, he returns to combat after swallowing some aspirin. Ernesto has just met a very charming revolutionary, the blonde Aleida March. She will become his second wife.

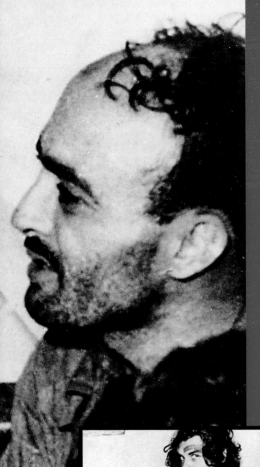

On December 31, 1958, the colonel of the provincial police surrenders. On January 1, the last garrison in Santa Clara lays down its arms.

During the New Year festivities, President Batista discreetly flees the country for Santo Domingo. The *libertadores* race toward the capital, preceded by their romantic and chivalrous legend.

No levantes himnos de victoria / En el día sin sol de la batalla.

("Do not sing hymns of victory on the sunless day of the battle.")

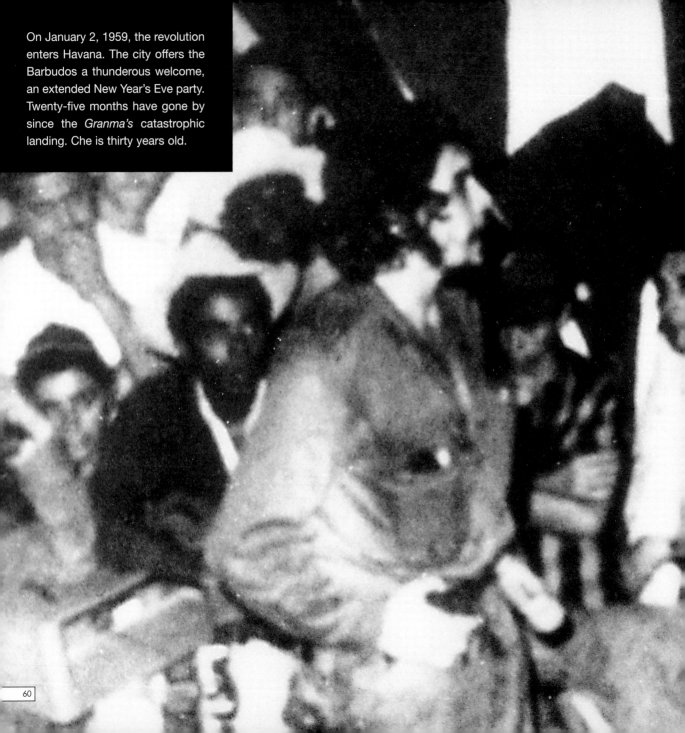

On January 2, 1959, the revolution enters Havana. The city offers the Barbudos a thunderous welcome, an extended New Year's Eve party. Twenty-five months have gone by since the *Granma's* catastrophic landing. Che is thirty years old.

"*I am not a libertador.*

Libertadores *do not exist.*

The people liberate themselves."

The Guevaras fly from Buenos Aires to be reunited with the son they haven't seen in six years.

A young beatnik had left them, and in his stead Che's parents find themselves reunited with a hardened hero celebrated by an entire people. **"He had transformed himself into a man** whose faith in the triumph of his ideas bordered on mysticism," his father later writes.

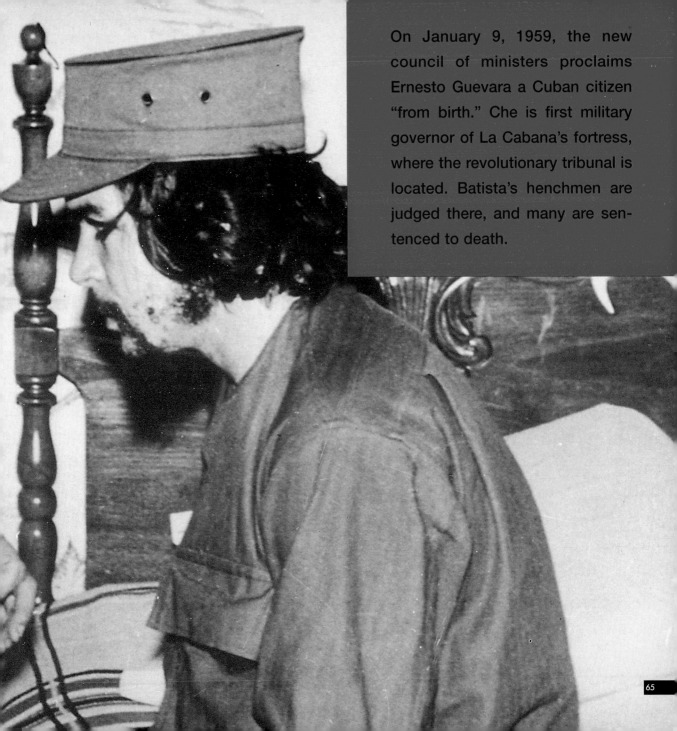

On January 9, 1959, the new council of ministers proclaims Ernesto Guevara a Cuban citizen "from birth." Che is first military governor of La Cabana's fortress, where the revolutionary tribunal is located. Batista's henchmen are judged there, and many are sentenced to death.

By the end of the 1950s, Cuba has become North Americans' favorite hangout. Scarcely 200 kilometers from Florida, Havana is a hotbed of prostitution where Meyer Lansky and Santos Traficante, two Mafia godfathers, reign. An Argentinean adventurer named Guevara now vows to expel gamblers, vice lords, and pimps. The United States controls 75 percent of Cuban commercial exchange. They also possess 90 percent of the country's mines and 50 percent of its land. In the capital, the middle class enjoys a lifestyle comparable to that of its northern neighbor.

Buicks and Chevrolets are parked in front of gleaming parking meters. On the other hand, 500,000 Cubans, out of a population of 6.5 million, are unemployed. In the countryside, only 4 percent of the sugarcane-cutters are able to eat meat; 2 percent, eggs. Nearly a quarter of the population is illiterate.

The new prime minister, Fidel Castro, proves that he is a nationalist and a reformist. He travels to the United States and meets then vice-president Richard Nixon, who believes he can pacify him. But the new Cuban government proclaims an agrarian reform law on May 17, 1959, which abolishes the latifundia, farms of more than 400 hectares. Public services such as telecommunications and transportation are nationalized, as are sugar and tobacco plantations. An ambitious social program is launched in the fields of health and education.

A banker like no other.

A joke, which soon becomes famous, spreads around the island. To Fidel's question—addressed at an assembly of militants: "Is there an economist in the room?"—the comandante Guevara raises his hand, believing to have heard, "Is there a communist?" "Very well, you shall be president of the Banco Nacional. . . ."

As a symbol of his disdain for money, Guevara signs the bills "Che."

The pretty *guerillera* Aleida March has not left Guevara's side since their first encounter in the Sierra Escambray, just before the battle at Santa Clara. Her allure, her intelligence and her militancy seduce the very man whose charm is as legendary as his military prowess. They marry in a private ceremony on June 2, 1959, and leave for a short honeymoon in a black Studebaker Ernesto had borrowed. As President of the National Bank, his salary is a mere $125 a month.

The first cargo of arms (from Belgium) that the Cubans have succeeded in acquiring, despite pressure from the Americans, arrives on March 4, 1960, in Havana port on board the French freighter *La Coubre*. But a tremendous explosion rocks the city. Attributed by the revolutionaries to the CIA, the attack leaves 75 of the port workers dead. A photographer of the magazine *Verde Olivo*, Gilberto Ande, discovers Che helping the wounded. Che does not allow him to take photographs. For Guevara, it is shameful to be the object of curiosity in such circumstances.

The day after, during a protest, Fidel denounces the attack and gives the order that is to become Cuba's motto: "the homeland or death." At the same time, the photographer of the daily *Revolución*, Alberto Korda, takes two photos of Che at the tribune. Years later, this cropped image will become a symbol for youth the world over.

"Che Guevara is part of the great myths of this century; his life is the story of our era's most perfect man."

Jean-Paul Sartre.

This same day in 1960, Jean-Paul Sartre and Simone de Beauvoir are among the crowd listening to Fidel Castro's speech. They have come to experience for themselves the Caribbean phenomenon that fascinates the world.

Relations with Washington continue to deteriorate. In response to the nationalization process, the Americans radically reduce their quota of sugar importations. This encourages an alliance with the Russians, who commit themselves to absorbing the sugar production. On October 19, tightening its stranglehold, the United States promulgates an embargo on commerce with the island.

"Cuba suddenly realized that all the consumer products on the island were produced in the States. The 'artificial' eggs that the housewives held in contempt for their runny yolk and medicinal taste carried the mark of North Carolina's farms on their shells, but some of the grocers washed this off with solvent and rubbed the eggs in chicken excrement so that they could be sold as local produce at a higher price."
Gabriel Garcia Marquez.

AN AMBASSADOR
IN ARMY FATIGUES

The revolution refuses to declare itself socialist until April 1961. However, the Cuban leadership was already leaning naturally toward the enemy of their arrogant neighbor, even before this date.

Che becomes Cuba's roving ambassador. Fidel charges him with the task of establishing economic relations with the socialist camp and the non-aligned states. Celebrated wherever he goes. he meets Nasser in Egypt, Tito in Yugoslavia, Nehru in India, Sukarno in Indonesia. In Moscow, with the enthusiasm of an explorer, Guevara signs commercial contracts which, he hopes, will keep the Americans from blackmailing their former Caribbean "colony."

Scornful of the polemics between the communist parties, Che Guevara continues his world tour via snow-covered Beijing, where he is received by Mao and Chou En-lai. Naturally, the Chinese compete with the Soviets in entertaining him. For Ernesto, who called his daughter "my little Mao," an old dream is turning into a reality. He does not, however, appreciate that, during a banquet in his honor, a little monkey is scalped in order to serve its brain while still warm.

Che believes that only industrialization will guarantee Cuba's political independence.

The task is colossal: "He worked from eight A.M. until four A.M. the next day," remembers Aleida, his wife, who adds that "along with his work at the ministry, and the articles and books he was writing, he also forced himself to study mathematics seventeen hours a week. . . ."

He spends his nights studying assiduously in his office, seated uncomfortably on the floor to avoid falling asleep.

Che urges the mechanization of the *zaffra,* the cutting of sugarcane. "One day," recounts the photographer Alberto Korda, "he decided to test the Alzadora, the first machine invented by Cuban engineers under his impetus. Just before taking the wheel, he turned to me and asked: 'Do you know how to cut cane with a machete? No. . . . Give him one so that he can contribute to the zaffra. . . .' I had to comply. He called this the 'baptism of fire.' . . ."

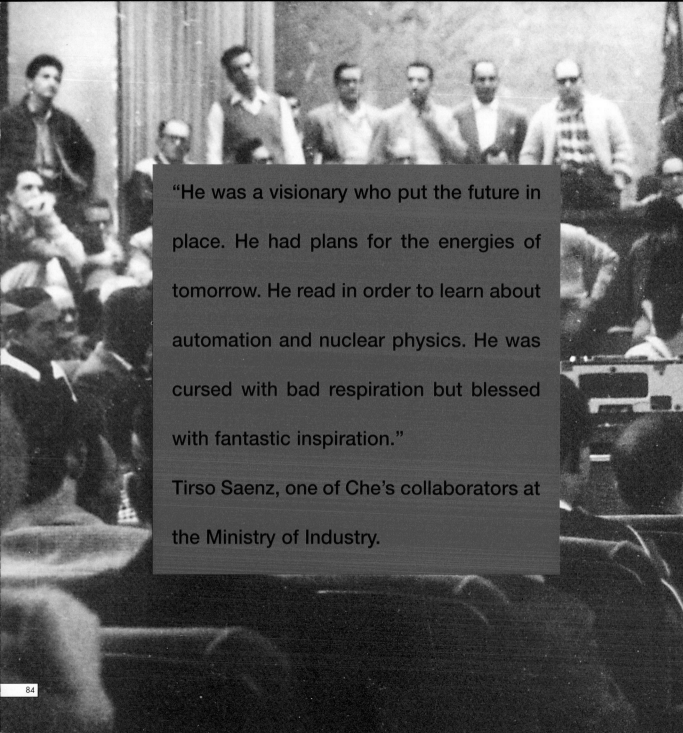

"He was a visionary who put the future in place. He had plans for the energies of tomorrow. He read in order to learn about automation and nuclear physics. He was cursed with bad respiration but blessed with fantastic inspiration."

Tirso Saenz, one of Che's collaborators at the Ministry of Industry.

"Les honneurs, ça m'emmerde!"
he declares in French.

El senor ministro prefers sweat and mud.

The new Minister misses the open air and physical exercise. To unwind, he plays baseball, Cuba's national sport. He also introduces Fidel Castro to golf, which he learned to play as a child.

Fidel invites Che and his mother to participate in the "Ernest Hemingway" fishing tournament,

but Guevara prefers to read and take photos rather than to tease swordfish.

"One must harden himself, but without ever losing his tenderness."

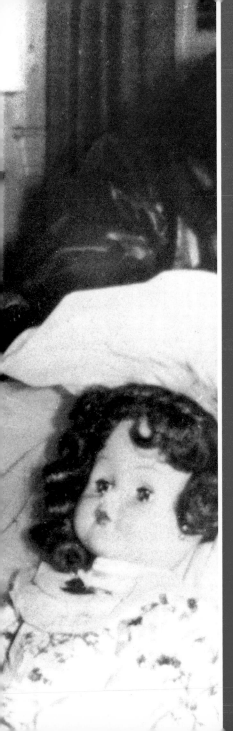

Hildita, the daughter he had with Hilda Gadea, is the eldest of Ernesto Guevara's children. Aleida March gives him four others: Aleidita, Camilo, Celia, and Ernesto.

Since the embargo, each Cuban family has the right to a few bottles of refresco to celebrate a birthday. In the early 1960s, some bottles of Coca Cola can still be found.

His father had taught him how to play chess at the age of six and remembers that, as an adolescent, Ernesto once reached a draw while playing against Argentinean chess master Miguel Najdorf. Che Guevara organizes a chess tournament at the Ministry of Industry with the Russian champion Victor Kortchnoï. In 1963, he plays by telephone with the future world champion, Bobby Fischer.

Che smokes too much: his colleagues at the Ministry worry about his health. He finally concedes by saying, *"All right, I'll cut down to one a day."*

The next morning, he arrives with a cigar nearly a meter long.

Hombre lobo, no!
Hombre nuevo, si!

("No to the wolf-man! Yes to the new man!")

Che Guevara establishes volunteer work as a semi-sacred act of the revolution.

He sets the example on Sundays, carrying sacks of sugar, building houses and harvesting sugarcane. Like a crusader, he is the incarnation of his dream of a "new man."

"Let me tell you, at the risk of sounding ridiculous, that the true revolutionary is guided by love. It is impossible to imagine an authentic revolutionary without this quality. This may be one of the great traits of the revolutionary leader. He must combine an impassioned spirit with a cold mind and be able to make painful decisions without flinching. . . . In these conditions, one has to have a lot of humanity and a great sense of truth and justice in order not to fall into extreme dogmatism . . . so as not to isolate oneself from the masses. Each day, one must struggle to transform this love for humanity into concrete facts and acts worthy of example."

The Cuban revolutionary is in New York on December 11, 1964. At the United Nations' tribune, his speech is violently "anti-Yankee." He also indirectly denounces the peaceful coexistence policy followed by the Kremlin: "Peaceful coexistence between nations does not exist between the exploiters and the exploited, between the oppressors and the oppressed."

Che looks ahead to the future: "When the moment arrives, I will be ready to die for the freedom of any Latin American country, without asking anything from anyone, without exploiting anyone, without expecting anything in return. . . ."

SHAME ON THE
CTORS
LUTION
RAVO
FIDEL
STRO
LONG LIVE
CUBAN
REVOLUTION
HAIL
FIDEL CAS
MAN OF
WELCO
TO
WELC
TO
OSAG
CHA

After New York, the revolutionary continues his voyage toward Africa. First Algeria, then Mali, Congo-Brazzaville, Guinea, Dahomey, Ghana, Tanzania, and Egypt. The Africans call him "Latin America's Mao." Upon his return to Algiers on February 24, 1965, Che makes a speech that criticizes anew the "egoism" of the Soviet Union's foreign policy. *"How can we speak of mutual benefit when we sell, at world market prices, raw materials produced by the sweat and limitless suffering of poor countries, and buy, at world market prices, machines produced by modern, automated factories?"*

Algerian president Ahmed Ben Bella—who was to be overthrown a few months later by Houari Boumediene—writes: "A non-commercial exchange has risen between Cuba and Algeria as a token of giving and solidarity. . . . We have given, but we have equally received. We never did any accounting. . . . This system of exchange greatly pleased Che as it was based on sincere friendship, which corresponded to his temperament."

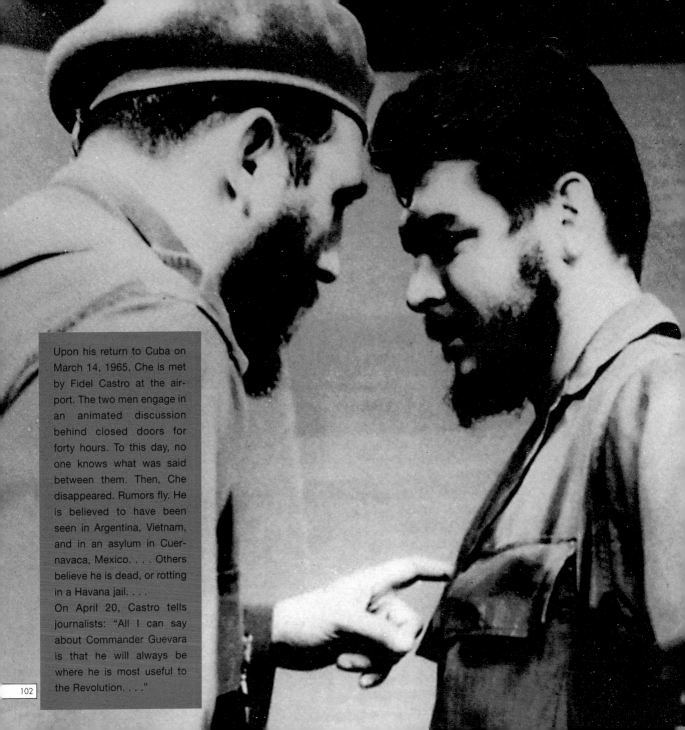

Upon his return to Cuba on March 14, 1965, Che is met by Fidel Castro at the airport. The two men engage in an animated discussion behind closed doors for forty hours. To this day, no one knows what was said between them. Then, Che disappeared. Rumors fly. He is believed to have been seen in Argentina, Vietnam, and in an asylum in Cuernavaca, Mexico. . . . Others believe he is dead, or rotting in a Havana jail. . . .

On April 20, Castro tells journalists: "All I can say about Commander Guevara is that he will always be where he is most useful to the Revolution. . . ."

Habana
Año de la agricultura

Fidel:

Me acuerdo en esta hora de muchas cosas, de cuando te conocí en casa de María Antonia, de cuando me propusiste venir, de toda la tensión de los preparativos.

Un día pasaron preguntando a quién se debía avisar en caso de muerte y la posibilidad real del hecho nos golpeó a todos. Después supimos que era cierto, que en una revolución se triunfa o se muere (si es verdadera). Muchos compañeros quedaron a lo largo del camino hacia la victoria.

Hoy todo tiene un tono menos dramático porque somos más maduros, pero el hecho se repite. Siento que

"Set-off two, three, many Vietnams."

As the world asks itself where he has disappeared to, Che Guevara is, in fact, attempting to ignite a new revolution in the heart of Africa.

A group of soldiers—all of them black—are assembled in Cuba in the barracks of Pinar del Rio. They know their leader only through these two photographs. They ask themselves who is this elegant, clean-shaven man with slicked back hair smoking Cohibas, Fidel Castro's favorite cigar. . .

In the former Belgian Congo, the people call Che *Muganda,* "he who relieves." For the guerrillas, he is Commander "Tatu." "I dream of creating an army that will bring victory to the Congolese."

But after eleven months, the operation is cut short due to the irresponsibility of the African revolutionaries, described by Guevara as "tourists [notably a certain Laurent Désiré Kabila] who prefer to lead a life of ease in the world's capitals." After a series of violent asthma attacks, dysentery and malaria, Che weighs less than fifty kilos. He is treated in Dar es-Salaam and then in Prague before returning secretly to Cuba.

FOTOGRAFIA DEL PORTADOR

Back on his feet, Guevara's ambition this time is to spread the fever of the revolution all over Latin America; to turn the Andes cordillera into an immense Sierra Maestra. He chooses Bolivia as the place to ignite the insurrection.

While the CIA believes him to be hospitalized in the Soviet Union, Guevara disguises himself, with the help of the Cuban secret service, as a graying, forty-year-old bourgeois. To create baldness, his hair is partly shaven off. To make him appear shorter, the heels of his shoes are hollowed out. Thick-lensed glasses and bushy eyebrows complete the effect.

Fidel examines Che's false papers. To facilitate his roundabout voyage, Guevara is furnished with two Uruguayan passports. The first is under the name Ramon Benitez Fernandez, businessman born in Montevideo on June 25, 1920 (eight years before the birth of Ernesto Guevara). The second, under the name Adolfo Mena Gonzalez.

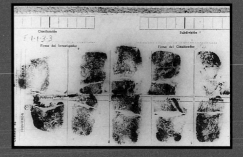

Self-portrait in a hotel room
at the Copacabana, La Paz.

The jeep rolls into a tree. When the driver recognized his bespectacled and hatted passenger, he could not help flinging his arms around Che's neck: "Coño, I know you like me but you're going to kill us before we even begin to fight!"

It is November 1966. Guevara, equipped with his false papers, has just arrived in La Paz, the Bolivian capital. The two men make their way southwest toward the Nancahuazu, the base chosen by the guerrillas, a remote region, hostile and deserted.

With only fifty men, eighteen of whom are loyal
Cubans, Guevara first aims to establish a training
camp From there, the *guerilleros* are meant to spread
a revolutionary network all over Latin America.

On November 7, 1966, he begins a diary using a
red notebook made in Germany. He organizes his
camp around an isolated house, the *calmina*. Food
and ammunition are hidden in tunnels dug by the
men. The climate is torrid, the trees stunted and
gray. Thorns rip clothes and scratch skin. The
insects are numerous—"the yaguasa, the jejen, and
the marigui." enumerates Che in his diary. "The
bites cause wounds. . . . My beard has begun to
grow. In about two months, I will be myself again."

Instead of supporting the little group, as expected, the Bolivian communist party dissuades potential candidates from joining the underground forces. Moscow is unwilling to disturb the peaceful coexistence established between the two world superpowers. Che is forced to hastily enlist people, some of whom soon desert and betray him. In March, the camp is occupied by the army while Che is on an exploratory mission. The "pure guerrilla" stage begins.

Heidi Tamara Bunke Bider, alias Laura Guttierez Bauer, Maria Aguilera, or Laura Martinez, called Tania, was born in Buenos Aires in 1937. She is the daughter of a Polish Jewess and a German who emigrated to Argentina but returned to Germany after the War.

She first meets Che as his interpreter in East Germany in 1959. Two years later, she moves to Cuba. In 1964, Guevara requests her to infiltrate Bolivia as a "mole." In the guise of an earnest pharmaceutical student, she manages to infiltrate the private circle of the presidential palace. Once Che is in Bolivia, she serves as his liaison officer between himself and the guerrillas. She's also the one who takes a young French philosophy professor and journalist, Régis Debray (known as "Danton" in the guerrilla movement), to Guevara, alias "Ramon."

RECOM

Se ofrece la s

Pesos bolivianos

nes de boliviano

gue vivo o mu

PENSA

ma de 50.000.-
Cincuenta millo-
), a quién entre-
rto, (Preferible-
uerrillero Ernesto
se sabe

7

OKTOBER

Régis Debray and an Argentinean guerrilla, Ciro Bustos, are captured. After a prolonged trial, the Frenchman will be condemned to thirty years in prison. Bustos yields when his family is threatened, and draws portraits of the guerrillas. Che and his men soon find themselves hunted by five thousand soldiers supervised by North American advisers. On September 7, 1967, seven of Che's men are killed. Guevara offers those who remain the opportunity to leave, as he knows there is no other way out. Only one man flees.

Che's diary ends on October 7. On the eighth, encircled by two groups of Bolivian rangers in the gorge of Churo, he is wounded in the leg and captured.

Leaning against two soldiers, the most wanted man in the world is made to walk, limping, to the little village of La Higuera, where he is imprisoned in the dirt-floored schoolhouse. The decision to do away with Che was made long before in Washington. Orders from the Bolivian President, General Barrientos, arrive at La Higuera on the morning of the ninth. A CIA agent, Félix Rodrìguez, has his picture taken with Che, somber, disheveled and in rags. This is the last photo taken of Che alive.

The body, riddled with bullets,
is tied to a helicopter runner
for its final journey.

When Che's body arrives in Vallegrande, his eyes are open. His remains are exhibited to the press on a washtub in a hospital laundry room. For the peasants, he is already *"San Ernesto de la Higuera."*

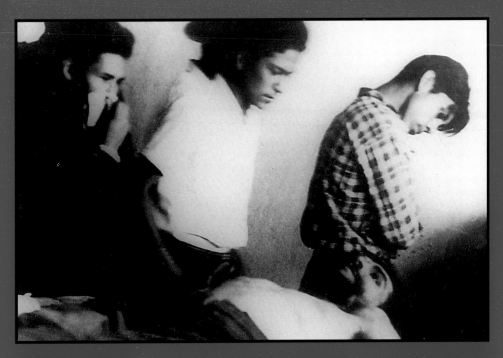

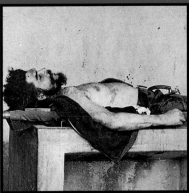

El Ch

e vive!

BIBLIOGRAPHY

Anderson, Jon L. *Che Guevara: A Revolutionary Life*. New York: Grove Atlantic, Inc., 1997.

Castaneda, Jorge. *Companero: The Life & Death of Che Guevara*. New York: Alfred A. Knopf, Inc., 1997.

Castro, Fidel. *Che: A Memoir by Fidel Castro*. Ed. David Deutschmann. New York: Ocean Press, 1994.

Castro, Fidel and Che Guevara. *To Speak the Truth: Why Washington's "Cold War" Against Cuba Doesn't End*. New York: Pathfinder Press, 1992.

Cooper, Mark. *Roll Over Che Guevara: Travels of a Radical Reporter Through the New World Order*. New York: W.W. Norton & Company, Inc., 1996.

Cupull, Adys, and Froilan Gonzalez. *Mission Bolivia: How the CIA Captured Che Guevara*. New York: Ocean Press, 1998.

Fernandez-Madrid, Felix. *Che Guevara & the Incurable Disease*. Pittsburgh, PA: Dorrance Publishing Company, Inc., 1997.

Guevara, Ernesto C. *A New Society: Perspectives for Today's World*. New York: Ocean Press, 1993.

———, *Bolivian Diary of Ernesto Che Guevara*. Trans. Michael Taber. New York: Pathfinder Press, 1994.

———, *Che Guevara & the Cuban Revolution: Writings & Speeches of Ernesto Che Guevara*. New York: Pathfinder Press, 1987.

———, *Che Guevara Speaks: Selected Speeches & Writings*. New York: Pathfinder Press, 1967.

———, *Episodes of the Cuban Revolutionary War, 1956-58*. Ed. Mary-Alice Waters. New York: Pathfinder Press, 1996.

———, *Guerilla Warfare*. Ed. Brian Loveman and Thomas M. Davies Jr. Lincoln, NE: University of Nebraska Press, 1985.

———, *Motorcycle Diaries: A Journey Around South America*. Trans. Ann Wright. New York: Routledge, Chapman & Hall, 1996.

———, and Fidel Castro. *Socialism & Man in Cuba*. New York: Pathfinder Press, 1989.

———, Carlos R. Rodriguez, Carlos Tablada, Jack Barnes, Steve Clark and Mary-Alice Waters. *Che Guevara, Cuba & the Road to Socialism*. New York: Pathfinder Press, 1991.

Guillermo, Cabera. *Memories of Che*. Trans. Jonathan Fried. New York: Carol Publishing Group, 1987.

Kellner, Douglas. *Ernesto "Che" Guevara*. Broomall, PA: Chelsea House Publishers, 1989.

Ramm, Hartmut. *The Marxism of Regis DeBray: Between Lenin & Guevara*. Lawrence, KS: University Press of Kansas, 1978.

Reynolds, Steve, and H.E. Carver. *The Murder of Che Guevara*. Hendersonville, TN: The Wild Geese Publishing Company, 1984.

Salmon, Gary. *The Defeat of Che Guevara: Military Response to Guerilla Challenge in Bolivia*. Westport, CT: Greenwood Publishing Group, Inc., 1990.

Tablada, Carlos. *Che Guevara Economics & Politics in the Transition to Socialism*, 2nd ed. New York: Pathfinder Press, 1990.

Taibo, Paco I. *Guevara, Also Known as Che*. New York: Saint Martin's Press, Inc., 1997.

Waters, Mary-Alice. *Che Guevara & the Fight for Socialism Today: Cuba Confronts the World Crisis of the '90s*. New York: Pathfinder Press, 1992.

ACKNOWLEDGMENTS

A lot of perseverance was needed for this Photobiography, imagined four years ago, to come into being. But this adventure has been a great pleasure. First because Che burns you. He touches in each of us a chord of moral insurrection, where faith in man, the energy which makes us believe despite all, is found. Secondly, because this book has given me the opportunity to meet marvelous people, most of whom have become friends: Alberto Korda, of course, my "agent in Havana," Raul Corrales. Perfecto Romero, Roberto Salas, the other photographers of Che, Maurice Hache, my accomplice, Olivier Nora, Marc Grinsztajn and Olivier Gravet, my editors. Paula and Paul Holme, Nathalie Nollet, Corina and Omar Castro, Florence Dorp, Karim Belkrouf, Marie-Christine Tiers, Jodi Lancelot, Caroline Nathalie, Leoniev and Marilo Leon, Miguel Marcano, our collaborators. Aleida March, Che's wife, who is director of the Centro de Estudios Historicos Che Guevara. Raul Roa Kouri, Cuba's ambassador to France, Pedro Alvarez Tabio (Oficina de Asuntos Historicos de Consejo de Estado, Havana), Fidel Aguirre, Jose Israel Morales, Bernardo Rodriguez Fernandez, Rolando Rodriguez (Editora Politica, Havana), Michel Antaki, Philippe Gielen (Le Cirque Divers, Liege), Olivier Binst (Planet, Paris), Adys Cupull and Froilan Gonzalez, Françoise Duboi-Sigmund, Felicia Boisne-Noc and Laurence Villa (Compagnie aérienne AOM), Ludovic Debrabander, Jean-Pierre Candas and Frédéric Radigois (PLD, Lille), Bertrand and Juliet Dufieux (Alliance Française, Havana), Mario Diaz (Fototeca de Cuba), the photographer José Figueroa, Martha Haya, Alicia Llarena (Biblioteca Nacional de Cuba), Una Liutkus and Antonio Vasquez (Havanatours, Paris), Lieutenant-Colonel Orencio Nardo Garcia, Abdel Romero, Elma Veitias (Museo de la Revolucion, Havana), Jose Antonio Martinez (Prensa Latina, Havana), Manuel Martinez Gomez (Bohemia, Havana), Eric Montfajon, Ana Ibis Fernandez, Marina Carchon (TOTAL, Havana), Colonel Morales Quevedo, Julio Cubria Vichot, Josefina Suarez (Editorial Capitan San Luis, Havana), Ana Maria Pellon Saez (OSPAAAL, Havana), Aracelys Reyes, Suarmis Rodriguez (Ministerio del Interior, Havana), Colonel Herman Wainshtok Rivas (Complejo de Museos Historicos-Militares, Havana). A special thought for Hildita Guevara, Che's eldest daughter, who died in August 1995.

—Christophe Loviny

Back cover
Guerilla and banker, writer and minister, "doctor without borders" and photographer, backpacker and ambassador: in 200 rare or unpublished photos, the "story of our era's most perfect man." (Jean-Paul Sartre).